12

PROFILES

Viv Richards

David Foot

Illustrated by
Susan Neale

Hamish Hamilton
London

Titles in the Profiles *series*

Edith Cavell	0-241-11479-9	The Queen Mother	0-241-11030-0
Marie Curie	0-241-11741-0	Florence Nightingale	0-241-11477-2
Roald Dahl	0-241-11043-2	Emmeline Pankhurst	0-241-11478-0
Thomas Edison	0-241-10713-X	Pope John Paul II	0-241-10711-3
Anne Frank	0-241-11294-X	Anna Pavlova	0-241-10481-5
Indira Gandhi	0-241-11772-0	Prince Philip	0-241-11167-6
Gandhi	0-241-11166-8	Beatrix Potter	0-241-12051-9
Basil Hume	0-241-11204-4	Lucinda Prior-Palmer	0-241-10710-5
Helen Keller	0-241-11295-8	Viv Richards	0-241-12046-2
John Lennon	0-241-11561-2	Barry Sheene	0-241-10851-9
Martin Luther King	0-241-10931-0	Mother Teresa	0-241-10933-7
Nelson Mandela	0-241-11913-8	Queen Victoria	0-241-10480-7
Bob Marley	0-241-11476-4	The Princess of Wales	0-241-11740-2
Montgomery of Alamein	0-241-11562-0		

First published 1987 by
Hamish Hamilton Children's Books
27 Wrights Lane, London W8 5TZ
© 1987 text by David Foot
© 1987 illustrations by Susan Neale
Cover photograph © Adrian Murrell/All Sport
All rights reserved
British Library Cataloguing in Publication Data
Foot, David, *1929—*
Viv Richards. — (Profiles).
1. Richards, Viv — Juvenile literature
2. Cricket players — Biography — Juvenile
literature
I. Title   II. Series
796.35'8'0924   GV915.R4/
ISBN 0-241-12046-2
Typeset by Pioneer
Printed in Great Britain at the
University Press, Cambridge

To the young cricket lovers
of St John's (Antigua), Taunton . . . .
and indeed everywhere else

Contents

1	A PROMISING TALENT	11
2	A BOOKMAKER'S BET	14
3	THE JOURNEY TO SOMERSET	21
4	'KING VIV'	27
5	WEST INDIES' HERO	31
6	TRIUMPHS AND TRIALS	35
7	CAPTAIN AT LAST!	43
8	A SENSE OF ADVENTURE	47
9	VIV LOOKS TO THE FUTURE	53
	Important Dates in Viv Richards' Career	57
	Viv Richards' Cricketing Achievements	58

Viv Richards

1 A Promising Talent

Many people had never heard of the small, delightful West Indian island of Antigua until Viv Richards emerged as one of the great post-war cricketers.

Isaac Vivian Alexander Richards was born on 7 March 1952. He lived with his parents and brothers in St John's, the capital of Antigua. His father, Malcolm, was a fine, well-built sportsman who played cricket for Antigua as an all-rounder and who also represented the Windward-Leeward team. Malcolm Richards was a man with authority in St John's who used to work as a warder at the local prison. He was made deputy chief warder before he retired. A popular and outward-going person, he had strong views on many things, including cricket.

Gretel Richards, Viv's mother, was a gentle, quiet woman. She was devoted to her family, but could sometimes be strict with her children, although never unreasonably so.

Both Viv's parents have had a strong influence on his life. They wanted him to have a good education and they first sent him to a private nursery school run by Mrs Ross. Later he went to St John's Boys' School and then Antigua Grammar School.

A keen football player

Whilst Viv was at school, he sang in the Cathedral choir at the three Sunday services. He liked the hymns, but often his mind strayed to the current Test Match and to such famous West Indian cricketers as Everton Weekes, Frank Worrell, and Clyde Walcott. Whenever the West Indians were on tour, Viv was never far from a crackling radio set.

Viv was bright, happy and intelligent, although he was not an outstanding scholar. His best subjects were history and religious knowledge, but he was always happiest on the sports field. When schoolfriends asked him what his ambitions were, he would reply, 'To play for Antigua at cricket and football.' Even then he was full of pride for his country.

Viv has always been a shy person and this was very evident during his childhood. The neighbours commented that he was very well-mannered, but that he didn't say much. His confidence grew, however, as soon as he went out to play cricket. His smile broadened and a spring came into his step. Several of his masters noticed the first signs of exceptional promise in his cricketing ability and began to encourage him. So too did his father and Pat Evanson, a former captain of Antigua, who lived opposite the Richards' home in St John's.

Before Viv left St John's Boys' School at the age of 11, he had scored his first century. He scored three more at the grammar school. When he was made captain of the school team he promoted himself to No.3 in the batting order, a position he kept for most of his career.

During this time, he also played plenty of beach cricket. Sometimes the hurriedly arranged matches were played on dreadful, improvised pitches. But no-one ever complained, despite the uneven bounce of the hard ball, and the lack of pads and bats. Uneven wickets sharpened the reflexes.

During the school holidays, Viv and his younger brother, Mervyn, staged their own five-match Test series, the West Indies against Australia or England. They would play all day long, one against one, to an imaginary crowd. Little did they know then, that within a few years, the shouts of the crowd would be real and Viv's dream of playing for his country would have become a reality.

2 A Bookmaker's Bet

Whilst Viv was at school, his approach at the crease tended to be far too impatient. Sports masters would shake their heads as he began taking liberties to try and build up early runs. He seemed to have all the shots, but he also wanted to try them out in the first over. His muscles had not yet developed and he was quite small-framed. Yet he made his school-mates whistle with admiration as he hooked and pulled, and hit the ball across the line.

His naturally free but impulsive batsmanship would often get him into trouble. He would give simple catches and suffer a reprimand in silence from the cricket master. Once or twice, he even found that he had been dropped from the school side for the next match.

In spite of this, everyone agreed that Viv was a quite remarkably gifted player. Uncoached he may have been, but he had such natural style and grace. When he was not trying to hit the ball into the sea, he looked so much better than any of his young team-mates. He had the rare ability of getting to the pitch of the ball; his timing was mature — and everyone marvelled at the power in his wrists.

Viv's early cricketing days were marred by an event which he bitterly regretted later. He was playing for Antigua against St Kitts. It was an important match for him. Six thousand spectators were expecting him to do well. Unfortunately he was out to a borderline catch at short-leg almost immediately. It was probably a bad decision, but that did not excuse Viv's behaviour. He argued and refused to go. At last, when he had calmed down, he left the field. After he had gone, hundreds of young spectators invaded the pitch. They held a demonstration and raised a banner which said, 'No Vivi — No Play'.

The match was held up for two hours whilst all kinds of advice was given to Viv. He returned to the crease, but was stumped without scoring. In the second innings he was out again for a duck. To be dismissed for three ducks in the same match was surely unique.

Even now, Viv thinks back to the match with a mixture of regret and embarrassment. As a result of his behaviour he was officially banned for two years.

Viv left school when he was 18 and started playing for a leading St John's club. His brother Donald was already a member. After a season Viv moved to another club called Rising Sun, where his friend Andy Roberts played. Andy was also soon to become a great West Indian player. He and Viv spent much of their time together, two quiet Antiguans who shared a great love of cricket. They often monopolised the honours for Rising Sun — Viv as batsman, Andy as bowler.

They were considered the most talented young sportsmen in St John's, although as yet they had had no formal coaching. The Voluntary Coaching Council of the island decided to give them the opportunity and send them to a famous school of coaching in London, Alf Gover's indoor cricket school.

They left the warmth of the Antiguan sunshine and arrived in England in the depths of winter. London was cold and dark. It was Viv's first time away from home, apart from a trip to Bridgetown in Barbados to see one day of a West Indies Test Match against New Zealand. That had been a trip to remember: Viv was introduced to Gary Sobers for the first time in his life and was given a pair of batting gloves by another fine player, Lawrence Rowe, as a keepsake.

At Alf Gover's school the boys were encouraged to build on their natural, instinctive skills. The coach tried to improve Viv's technique against the ball that swung away and against the off-spinner. They talked about his grip and his open stance. Years later, Mr Gover recalled, 'He was a modest lad and a pleasure to coach. It was obvious to me he had a touch of class, of the kind that leads to great batting.'

When their daily coaching was over, the two Antiguans felt very alone in London. They went to the cinema occasionally in the evenings. But the highlight of their stay was when they went to Highbury to watch Arsenal Football Club play against Leeds United.

On Viv's return to Antigua, his cricketing progress continued. In 1971, and still not yet 20, he made his debut for the Leeward Islands. He could think of nothing else but cricket. His parents, who were responsible and loving, were becoming just a little

Viv's parents, Malcolm and Gretel Richards

anxious about him. His father pressed him to give his future some thought.

Viv's first job after he left school was as a waiter at Darcy's Bar and Restaurant in St John's. The owner was very keen on cricket, and he willingly gave Viv time off to play. Viv's quiet charm and polite manner earned him plenty of generous tips, but in his heart he knew that it wasn't the right job for him.

In the meantime, his father was thinking about sending Viv to New York. Malcolm Richards had family links there, as his mother had been born in New York. He felt that it would be a good idea for Viv to go there to study for a qualification in electrical engineering at night-school. That, at least, seemed to offer more security for the future than a decidedly uncertain career as a part-time waiter or an unpaid cricketer.

Viv accepted his father's argument and he thought seriously about a livelihood. The glamour of New York appealed to him, but he was reluctant to give up cricket. He had recently progressed to the Shell Shield matches with the Combined Islands, and he had also met West Indian cricketing friends back from seasons in the county championship or the cricket leagues in England. There was even a strong rumour that Viv might go to England, to play in the league for Oldham. 'You'd like that more than electrical engineering and all that studying at night,' his friends told him.

Viv knew he had to choose between cricket and a 'proper' career. He also knew that he had to make up his mind quickly; he owed that to his parents. Then, suddenly and unexpectedly, his problem was solved for him.

A bookmaker from England arrived in Antigua in early April 1973, on holiday with his wife. Len Creed came from Somerset; cricket was his passion and he was also the Vice-Chairman of Somerset County Cricket Club.

He had come to Antigua on a tour with a West Country cricket team. He had also planned to do a little talent-scouting. In his pocket, he carried a crumpled cutting from a sports magazine. It was a recommendation from Colin Cowdrey, the famous England batsman, about a very 'promising' young player whom he had

Viv with Len Creed

seen on a visit to the West Indies twelve months earlier. The player's name was Viv Richards.

The story of Len Creed's discovery has been told many times since then. Creed watched as the English touring party played Antigua and a very nervous Richards was stumped almost first ball. But 'Nookie', the square-leg umpire knew what was at stake and shook his head. Viv stayed in, fielded far more brilliantly than he batted, and earned the Somerset Vice-Chairman's approval.

The difficulty for Len Creed was to convince the other Somerset officials, by a long-distance telephone call, that he had discovered an emerging genius. Finally he proposed that he would pay for Viv's trip to England himself and look after him for twelve months. If Viv was good enough, Creed would be paid back. If not, Viv would return to Antigua.

It was agreed. The rumours spread rapidly around St John's: 'Vivi's off to England.' Viv, his head in a whirl, packed his bag and headed for the airport. It was goodbye to those plans for night-school studies. He was not quite sure what he was letting himself in for. Cricket for a living? Everything was too good to be true; there had to be a catch.

3   The Journey to Somerset

Full of anticipation, Viv arrived at Heathrow. But problems were awaiting him; he had no work permit. For a few dreadful hours he faced the possibility of being put on the next plane back to the Caribbean. Eventually, everything was sorted out. Viv was tired, hungry and apprehensive, as he left Heathrow for Bath.

'Now don't worry, trust me,' said Len Creed. 'It will take you the whole of this summer to qualify for Somerset. They haven't said definitely that they will take you — but they will.' In the meantime, Viv began playing for Lansdown, one of the better local club sides. His first match was for the Second XI on 23 April 1973. The wicket was as soft as a pudding and not at all like the hard wickets that Viv was used to. In spite of this, he was still batting at the end of the match and won the game with two ferocious sixes. After that he always played for Lansdown's first team.

As a means of earning some pocket money, Viv helped the groundsman at Lansdown. During the week Viv rolled the square and cut the outfield.

To start with, it was only natural that he felt lonely and rather homesick. He missed the parties and calypso music of home and he found the way of life in England very different. Gradually, however, Viv got used to it all. His colleagues in the cricket club made him feel very welcome.

The season was progressing well for Lansdown. Viv would regularly beat the opposition almost single-handedly. For instance, he scored two hundreds against Trowbridge Cricket Club. Some of the Trowbridge players felt that he shouldn't have been allowed to play — he was too good for their class of cricket!

Viv still missed the hard, true wickets of Antigua. As the English wickets were so different, he was advised to change his style slightly and concentrate more on the front foot. In England, it was never easy for him to lean back and hook, in the way he did so freely in St John's.

Viv's reputation as a 'hurricane hitter' grew during the season. Every week his name was in the headlines of the local papers. Members of Somerset were following his progress with growing interest. Nevertheless Viv knew that there was no guarantee that he would end up playing as a county cricketer.

During that season he was also invited to the nets at Taunton, the Somerset headquarters. The county coach, Tom Cartwright, watched Viv's game critically, and was much impressed. He probably wished to see Viv playing more cautiously. But Viv's feet were usually in the right place and he got to the pitch of the ball. Who would deter a player with such a stylish and entertaining approach?

'Well, what do you think?' asked a beaming Len Creed.

'We shall have to see how he fares in good-class competitive cricket,' came Cartwright's reply. West Indian players had a reputation for swinging the bat, but not all of them had the determination and technique to succeed on English wickets.

Viv was selected to play for Somerset's Under-25 side against Gloucestershire. This was considered a real test for him, more challenging than Saturday afternoon cricket. The Somerset committee was present in force to assess Viv's ability. He rose to the challenge and responded by scoring a century.

At this time Viv still lacked self-confidence, no matter how well he was making runs. When he was alone, he would often think about his future. He still didn't know if he would be asked to stay and play for Somerset.

The club studied the reports about Viv from former county players and the coach. It was not a difficult choice to make: Viv was offered a two-year contract. His terms, as an uncapped player, were modest, but his joy at the news was considerable. He rolled the Lansdown square for the last time, looked disapprovingly at the blisters on his hands, hammered another hundred for the club side and flew home.

His family, girlfriend Miriam, and old schoolfriends were waiting for him. 'I've made it!' he told them shyly. 'Somerset are taking a chance with me.'

He returned to Taunton for the start of the 1974 season. He was introduced to the other players and given his new kit. Viv walked alone, full of wonder, across the ground. He liked what he saw; there was a cosy feel to it. The boundary appeared temptingly

'Firm friends' — Ian Botham and Viv Richards

short. It was made for sixes.

Viv had already heard much about Somerset's captain, Brian Close, who had recently come down from Yorkshire to play for Somerset. He seemed to Viv to expect the team to be extremely disciplined; he told them exactly what he expected from them. 'You're all a bit soft and easy going down in the West Country. You aren't used to winning anything. I want to change all that,' he said.

Viv moved into the club flat alongside the ground. He shared it with two other players. One was also a newcomer to county cricket that season. His name was

Ian Botham. He and Viv immediately became firm friends.

The first match of the season was against Glamorgan at Swansea, in the Benson and Hedges competition. Viv did not expect to be selected, but Brian Close said to him, 'You're in; you'll be batting at No.4.' Viv was thrilled to be chosen but, on the car journey through Wales, the nagging self-doubts returned.

He need not have worried. Somerset won and Viv earned the Gold Award for an undefeated 81. As Viv returned to the pavilion, Close asked the players to

Viv with Brian Close

line up and applaud the newcomer. Len Creed, the hardened bookie, was in tears. Close put his arm around Viv's shoulders and said, 'You'll do for me, and Somerset have found a great player for the future.'

On the car journey back to Taunton, the young West Indian was in high spirits. He had gone for his shots and almost everyone had approved. He had been accepted by a famous England player, Brian Close. The conversation bubbled with congratulations.

'You'll like Somerset, it's the right county for you. You're an entertainer and a big hitter, you don't hang around. The supporters down in Taunton, Bath and Weston-super-Mare have always loved players like you,' Viv was assured. The sad events of 1986 were a long way ahead.

4 'King Viv'

Viv Richards was an instant success with Somerset. The crowds liked his boyish grins and modest manner. They found it hard to believe that he was still quite inexperienced when it came to playing on England's green wickets, where the ball moved late off the seam. Viv, an intelligent cricketer, had learned to adjust his technique. It would have been disastrous for him if he had assumed that every wicket would be as true and reliable as those he had left behind in Antigua. 'Don't forget, I served a useful apprenticeship, too, on some of those rough, improvised strips of pasture land which we used for our schoolboy matches,' he would say.

After his Gold Award at Swansea, Viv scored two hundreds against Gloucestershire and Yorkshire in that opening championship season of 1974. He was awarded his county cap, and soon fans were calling him 'King Viv'. This newly-acquired title was chanted with delight whenever he was at the wicket.

It was not simply that he was scoring plenty of runs, it was the style with which he was scoring them. His approach was always entertaining. Many of the runs came from boundaries, although he never resorted to sheer slogging. His cover drive was so perfect that it

The graceful batsman

was already being compared with that of such past
great players as Walter Hammond and Jack Hobbs. A
few Somerset supporters were a little shocked at the
way Viv would push forward to a ball on his off stump
and send it to the mid-wicket boundary. It wasn't a shot
that was in the coaching manual. Yet he still made it
look attractive.

Viv's form for Somerset was quietly noted by the
West Indies team selectors. They had also been
impressed with his batting in the West Indian Shell
Shield Tournament, in which he had taken part before

leaving for England. To Viv's genuine astonishment, he was selected to go on the 1974-75 West Indies tour of India, Pakistan and Sri Lanka. Viv admitted later, 'It was the biggest surprise of my life; I didn't think I had any chance at all. The honour thrilled and then frightened me. Would I be good enough?'

It was a very self-conscious 22-year-old who joined his more famous West Indian colleagues on the flight to India. Viv's confidence was boosted briefly when he scored a hundred in the first warm-up match of the tour. But it was shattered after his Test Match debut at Bangalore. He was very nervous and struggled to cope with the skill of the Indian spinners on a drying wicket. In the first innings he was out for four; in the second he was out for three.

Viv has always been acutely self-critical and batting failures fill him with despair. He was inconsolable after such a miserable introduction to Test Match cricket. But the captain, Clive Lloyd, a good friend and a fatherly figure, assured Viv that there was no likelihood that he would be dropped from the team on the evidence of one bad performance. Later in the tour, Viv responded by scoring a marvellous 192 not out at Delhi.

It was at Delhi too that there was a particularly unpleasant incident during a match. Clive Lloyd had scored a splendid double century and the series was in the balance: either side could win. Spectators ran on to the field to congratulate Lloyd and the local police over-reacted. There were some dreadful scenes and 90 minutes of play were lost. It even led to hastily called meetings between the cricket officials and State ministers.

Viv must have wondered what Test cricket was all about when, in the following Test series against Pakistan, there were far worse scenes in Karachi. Hundreds of spectators invaded the pitch and the military police used batons. 'We made for cover, I can tell you,' Viv told his friends later.

On his return to England, Viv's career continued successfully. The big scores mounted and the cricket historians followed his development with great interest. In Antigua too, his girlfriend Miriam was also watching his progress, keeping a scrapbook full of news-cuttings about him. Viv would set himself targets whilst he was at the wicket and he could not disguise his joy when the runs came freely. The bad memories of his first West Indian tour quickly faded.

Those were still happy and carefree days with Somerset. He enjoyed the small-town atmosphere of Taunton. He tried fish and chips for the first time and liked them. Back in his flat, he played his records and cassettes. He was always very interested in clothes and was considered one of the most fashionable dressers in the town. He made many friends. At that time, he and Hallam Moseley were the only West Indians in the Somerset team and they were both immensely popular.

Viv's cricket was progressing. He had been on his first overseas tour with the West Indies and he was playing well for Somerset. Life was sweet indeed.

5   West Indies' Hero

It must surely be the ambition of all fine cricketers to play for their country and ultimately to captain it. Viv was no exception. By the age of 22, he had already played with the West Indies against India, but would his career with the team stop there?

In fact, it was to continue with the West Indies 1975-76 tour of Australia. During this tour, Viv quickly learned that cricket at international level could be tough and competitive. One or two of the Australian bowlers, for instance, were clever at trying to threaten opposing batsmen. 'They didn't frighten me,' said Viv. 'It made me that bit more determined to succeed against them.'

However the tour was not a success for the West Indians: they lost 5-1. When such a team fails in a series, the cricket board want to know the reasons why. It led to reports about a lack of team spirit and discipline.

The story was very different during the 1976 West Indies tour of England. By then, Viv had become a key member of the West Indies side, despite the occasional run of low scores. Many cricket fans called him the best batsman in the world. Others compared his batting skill with Barry Richards, the South African who then

The bowler's nightmare

played for Hampshire. Viv was also dubbed 'a second George Headley'. He was embarrassed by such titles; he always shrank away from too much praise.

The England bowlers despaired; Viv kept attacking them wherever they pitched the ball. They asked one another: 'How do you bowl to this bloke? He just murders you!'

One could understand how they felt. Viv finished the tour with an average of more than 118. He scored double centuries against England at Trent Bridge and the Oval. It was quite remarkable that he managed to score his memorable 291 runs in the last match, as he should have been suffering from lack of sleep. He had scored 130 not out by the end of one day's play and retired for a good night's sleep at a leading London hotel. It seemed however, that every one of his relatives in England had come to see him, along with half the population of Antigua, apparently on holiday here. They all crowded joyfully into his hotel room, offering their congratulations and breaking into song. Even the son of Antigua's Prime Minister knocked on the door. Viv, tired and happy, got to sleep in the early hours of the morning. He was still able to take his score to nearly 300 the following day. One of his team-mates joked, 'If only he'd been allowed to get to sleep, we should have seen 500 from him!'

In 1978 Viv's cricket for the West Indies came to a temporary halt as he played for Kerry Packer's World Series Cricket which threatened to revolutionise the game. Viv had consulted Clive Lloyd and other trusted colleagues before deciding to join the Series. Feelings ran high about the project. There were angry words from those who claimed that many of the top players had shown disloyalty in choosing to earn high salaries from Kerry Packer.

It all seems a long time ago now. But Viv and the other cricketers who played for Packer have no regrets. They played some thrilling cricket, despite the artificial conditions of playing under floodlights with white balls. Many cricketing authorities decided to impose bans on the players who appeared in World Series Cricket. In spite of all the arguments, Viv felt that the Series gave him another opportunity to take on the best players in the world.

Back with the West Indies after the ban had been lifted, Viv remained the dashing hero. He was the stroke-maker who could turn the match around on his own; the giant who refused to be unsettled by great bowlers' reputations. He was the record-breaker who, when the mood was right, threatened to do the impossible.

6 Triumphs and Trials

Viv had been missed by Somerset during those summers when he was playing for the West Indies. On his return to Somerset, he brought back with him the sparkle and extra element of excitement that had been lacking in the side. During the 1977 season, he scored seven flowing centuries for his county. At Bristol, Hove and Weston-super-Mare he went on to score double centuries. On occasions it looked as if no bowler in the world would ever get him out. Yet he was prepared to take risks. Because of the way he played cricket, he did give the bowler a chance — although in view of his technique, it was often a slight one!

During this time, Viv was maturing as a person. Brian Close, with whom he often travelled on away trips, reprimanded him for hasty and unwise shots. Close kept the Somerset fielders, including Viv, on their toes. But there was also laughter and relaxation in the dressing room. Richards got on well with the other players. They joked about the late hours he kept and his apparent lack of sleep. It was not unusual to see him curled up in a dark corner of the changing room between innings.

That year, 1977, Somerset beat the Australians for

Celebration!

the first time in 22 meetings since 1893. It was Joel Garner's first match for the county and the young West Indian took a wicket in his first over. Those were heady days for Somerset. The crowds were larger than ever before and this county side, unglamorous and unsuccessful for so many years, was now one of the most discussed teams in the country. The thrilling development of Richards and Botham, side by side, was very much part of Somerset's new-found success.

Yet something was missing — a title. 'Win us one, Viv,' the fans used to say. He tried hard and failed in 1978. The county lost the Gillette Cup final to Sussex on the Saturday and the John Player title to Essex on the Sunday. Spirits were very low in the Somerset dressing room after the Sunday match. Most of the players, including Viv, were in tears.

The following year, however, Somerset's fortunes turned. On the last Saturday of the season they won the Gillette Cup. It was a match in which Viv scored a wonderfully composed and responsible 117. The next day Somerset won the John Player League; Viv had bowled extremely well. Somerset had won something at last.

The club went on to win the Benson and Hedges Cup in 1981, a year which was also to be good for Viv personally. On 24 March 1981, he and Miriam were married. It seemed as if the entire population of Antigua were present at the wedding, both in the church and in the surrounding streets. For the few who stayed at home, the marriage service was broadcast on national radio. There was a speech from the Prime

Viv and Miriam on their wedding day

Minister. It is not surprising that Viv was too shy to say anything at the reception.

Viv was able to give Miriam a very special wedding present. A few days after his marriage, he played in Antigua's first official Test Match against England. Everyone guessed that Viv wanted the match to be a memorable occasion. He made the crowd deliriously happy by scoring a century.

His innings was as intriguing as it was historic. Viv scored his opening 50 runs at breakneck speed, and then slowed down. He became oblivious of everything as he willed himself to reach three figures. The acclaim was tremendous. Nothing could have been more moving. Later, Viv admitted, 'Not my best hundred . . . but my most important and emotional.'

It was surely the climax of his richly talented career to date. As a boy he had dreamed that he would actually see Test cricket on his beloved Recreation Ground, where once his father used to help prepare the wicket. Now it had happened. And Viv had been the century-maker, the romantic hero.

In the same year, he led the Combined Islands team to victory in the Shell Shield Tournament for the first time ever in the team's history. This was yet another honour that Viv could share with his fellow Antiguans.

Miriam and Viv both liked children, and it was not long before their daughter, Matara, was born. Their son, Mali, was born two years later.

Back in England, Viv helped Somerset win the Natwest Trophy in 1983. He was always considered to be the match winner in advance, and he rarely failed on the big occasion. During this year, Viv captained Somerset for the first time when Ian Botham was not available.

However, the constant strain of playing all year round, for county and country, season after season, was evident at times. Viv began experiencing lean times

A historic Shell-Shield victory

with Somerset and was occasionally caught out having hit tired, uncharacteristic shots. In 1985, to the dismay of the team members, the county finished bottom of the table. But who could say Viv had failed them, having scored nine hundreds that summer? When Somerset had played Warwickshire at Taunton that year, he had made 322. It was the highest individual score in Somerset's history.

Viv also stood in again as captain during that year.

Spectators at Taunton and elsewhere noticed that he enjoyed the responsibility. On the whole, he made the right decisions over declarations and the switching of bowlers. When Botham resigned for the 1986 season, it was thought by many that Viv would be appointed captain. Peter Roebuck was chosen instead. Some people believed Viv's heart was never in the game to quite the same extent for Somerset again. He denies this. 'I try all the time; maybe people expect too much.'

By his own dazzling standards, his form during the 1986 season was disappointing. He looked edgy and preoccupied. His expression was sombre. The spring had gone out of his step. Viv had a poor season, perhaps because he sensed that sweeping changes were about to be made to the team. The atmosphere in the dressing room was not particularly relaxed.

The Somerset management decided to start rebuilding the team. Viv's and Joel Garner's contracts were not renewed for the following season. Some thought this was a brave and progressive move. Others claimed that it was a dreadful mistake to get rid of the West Indians' finest batsman and one of their finest bowlers. Fellow club member Ian Botham certainly thought so and left the club in sympathy. The county appeared to be torn in half. At an important meeting attended by nearly 3,000 club members, it was eventually agreed that the management's decision was the correct one for the future of Somerset cricket.

Viv was shattered. His pride was greatly hurt. He had been largely responsible for the remarkable improvement in Somerset's fortunes, particularly when the county had finally won its first title after 104 years. He argued that he was being shown a complete lack of loyalty. Somerset, however, pointed out that they had always treated him well, and that he had had a successful benefit year with them in 1982.

Viv Richards, the cricketer who normally kept his inner thoughts to himself, was very angry. He appeared on television and spoke of betrayal, saying he felt like 'a workhorse being shot in the back'. His sense of injustice was acute. An important era had come to a bitter end.

7 Captain at last!

The relationship between the West Indies cricket board and the Test players has not always been an easy one. Viv, in particular, has had good reason to view the board with some caution.

Most people thought that when Clive Lloyd retired from the captaincy of the West Indies, Viv Richards would be the automatic choice as his successor. No one in top class cricket was more inspiring, more entertaining. At home in Antigua he was considered a hero. He was a match-winner; he could tame and then demoralise the very best bowlers.

Viv was liked and respected by his West Indian team-mates. He was never a selfish player and he always believed that team success was more important than individual achievement. He played cricket in a way that brought great excitement to the game. As a fielder he was brilliant, whether in the slips, the covers or the outfield. His joy was infectious as he shared in the triumphs of his team. Who will ever forget his obvious delight when he ran out three Australians in the final of the first World Cup held in England in 1975?

'What a match that was. It started at eleven in the morning and went on until a quarter to nine at night.

The brilliant fielder

The English crowds had been fairly reserved up to that point, but cricket, with the special thrill of international one-day contests, will never be the same again,' he later said.

However, when it was time for Clive Lloyd to step down from the captaincy, Viv's appointment was not announced as expected. Instead, Lloyd was asked to stay on for the time being. Viv remained silent. He was almost certainly hurt and asked himself privately what he had done wrong. Was it his fiery temperament? Was it that some of the cricket board members saw him as a rebel against authority? Did they feel the added responsibility would affect his form? Did he have too much of an independent streak? Did they wonder whether he would be able to cope with the speeches and the official appearances expected of a captain, knowing that he was naturally shy and did not really enjoy formal occasions?

There were also veiled suggestions that not all the board members approved of Viv's friends in the Rastafarian movement. Some of his old schoolfriends were Rastafarians and he was not unsympathetic to their beliefs. 'No one will choose my friends for me. I like to think that above all else I am a loyal person,' he said.

Eventually, the board made Viv captain of the West Indies team and he led them against New Zealand during the 1984-85 tour. In Antigua, long-standing admirers were delighted by the news. Viv took on the job with enthusiasm and an encouraging amount of skill.

He showed a gift for lifting spirits and pointing out what was expected of each member of the team. He was helpful to the younger players. When they struggled for form, he would say, 'Remember the difficult time I went through on my first tour of India.'

In captaining the West Indies, Viv had one obvious advantage: he had the benefit of the finest group of fast bowlers in the world. At the same time, he realised that there would soon be a need to rebuild the team to replace some of the older men. Did the West Indies have another batch of brilliant players coming along to take the place of Joel Garner, Michael Holding and Gordon Greenidge? Would supporters be expecting too much from a gradually changing Test team?

For a long time, the West Indians had been, without doubt, the greatest cricketing team in the world. None could match the brutal pace of their attack or the rich talents of their stroke-makers. But for how much longer? Viv knew that as captain there would be added responsibilities during this uncertain period.

It may prove increasingly difficult to be the captain of the West Indies if the team loses a little of its edge and its glamour. Viv has already shown, however, that he is willing to accept the challenge. 'I like leading my country. It's a great honour and it reflects favourably on my homeland of Antigua.'

8   A Sense of Adventure

What has made Vivian Richards such a great and exciting cricketer? Has it been the result of sheer grinding practice in the nets day after day? How much has Viv had to work at improving his technique?

It is unquestionable that he is a natural batsman. He has had advice at times from well-meaning people, such as Alf Gover, his father, neighbours and school-teachers. But the extraordinary fact is that Viv has become one of the greatest cricketers in the world, with very little coaching. He does what comes naturally; in his case, getting to the pitch of the ball and hitting it very hard indeed.

He is not against coaching, although he is critical of those cricket instructors who attempt to mould every young player in exactly the same way. He believes a coach should never try to curb natural ability. Viv has no time, however, for the cocksure cricketers who consider themselves to be above advice.

When he first went to Somerset, Viv knew that there were various weaknesses in his game. As he had been stronger on the leg side, he improved his off-side shots, and tightened his defence. Brian Close said of Viv: 'What I admired about him was that he was so eager to learn. He was a good listener.'

Fortunately, no one tried to make him a slower, less entertaining batsman. The rate of his scoring was a large part of his appeal. And even when he was racing along, the shots remained attractive and stylish. Apart from the occasional one-day matches, when everyone was expected to slog and make ugly strokes, his batting

The entertaining batsman

was a model to the hundreds of cricketing fans who went along to watch.

One of his most valuable natural assets is his exceptional eye sight. It has allowed him to pick up the line of the ball and to get into the right position earlier than anyone else in present-day cricket. As a result, he always seems to have plenty of time to play his shots. He uses his feet well, and his perfect timing makes it possible for him to penetrate the fielders and score all those boundaries.

And what about those shots of Viv's that no one will find in the coaching books — shots that make the spectators gasp and a few old cricket masters shake their heads in disapproval or wonder? In one such shot, he moves away to leg from his wickets and then sends a fantastic six over extra cover. If you ask him about it he grins with a trace of guilt, 'I make space for myself and risk leaving my stumps exposed. But I promise you I only go for that one in limited-overs cricket.'

Another example of an unorthodox shot that Viv has made famous, is when he turns a good-length delivery on his middle-and-off or off stump through mid-wicket. Very few coaches will advise their pupils to try their luck with that shot. Nor, in fact, will Viv. 'But the truth is I've always played it and it has brought me a lot of runs. The secret is to make sure you get to the pitch of the ball.'

This tells much about Viv. He is never afraid to do what comes naturally. There is nothing wrong in occasionally straying from the coaching book if it brings

A good teacher

you success. 'If you start taking a few liberties and they don't come off, then go back to basics and play it by the book,' he says with just the hint of a wink.

Playing for his country around the world, Viv has often faced and conquered some of the fastest and most fearsome bowlers of all time. He never flinched when standing up to the Australian demons, Dennis Lillee and Jeff Thomson. Nowadays, professional cricketers protect themselves more and more against the dangers of the very fast bowlers. Viv has always worn the minimum of protective gear, but he advises young cricketers to take sensible precautions.

He enjoys talking to young cricketers about the game. His message is always the same. He tells them to play with both a sense of enjoyment and adventure. But while he encourages them to have fun, he underlines the value of being competitive and trying to win.

Fitness is important to him. In Antigua he has spent hours jogging on the powder-white beaches. He continues to push himself hard in training. When he has been troubled with injuries and illness, he acts quickly on medical advice.

As for his emphasis on enjoyment, it shows in the way he holds his catches, the way he races round the outfield, and the way he returns the ball from the boundary. He enjoys bowling, and is willing to come on as a medium-pace or off-spin bowler.

His sense of adventure is obvious when he dares take the occasional risk. He often gives the opposing bowler just the suggestion of a chance and then refuses to bat predictably.

A world-class cricketer

When Viv is at his most flowing and relaxed, he is
still one of the truly great and timeless world-class
batsmen. From that wonderfully still and comfortable
stance, he erupts to reveal the magic and might of his
wrists with some of the most gloriously attacking shots
ever invented.

9 Viv Looks to the Future

In March 1987, Viv celebrated his thirty-fifth birthday. He is still a fine figure, broad of shoulder and firm of muscle, and still capable of scoring many exciting runs. Provided his enthusiasm does not wane, his value to the West Indian cricket team is going to be greater than ever.

When Viv left Somerset in 1986, he had offers of contracts from Australia and clubs in the cricket league in England. He talked over his future with Ian Botham, who had also suddenly changed direction and allegiances. With genuine sadness, Viv considered selling his house in Taunton, his family's second home. But in the end, he caused some surprise by deciding to play for the Lancashire League club, Rishton, during 1987.

Viv has, however, come to the stage in his life when he needs to give some thought to a future career. He has considered building up business interests in both the property market and the fashion industry. There will, no doubt, be scope for him to continue present sponsorship deals.

He has often talked of supervising a coaching school for promising young cricketers in Antigua, giving encouragement and guidance, and helping to make sure that the island provides many future Test players. He would dearly love to be able to give something back to the sporting life of his native land. From his early days as a first-class cricketer, he sponsored a basketball team in St. John's. He has also given unpublicised financial help to individual young cricketers.

Some believe that Viv might enter into the world of politics. But he also feels passionately about moral issues. He is very proud of being a West Indian and will not tolerate racial prejudice. There have been several incidents when he has been provoked. One was at Harrogate where Viv, limping with an ankle injury, had just been run out. On his unhappy stroll back to the pavilion, a Yorkshire supporter made a racist remark. The cricketer's response was to walk in the direction of the comment and ask who had said it. His eyes were blazing. No one admitted to uttering the insult. In frustration, Viv stormed into the pavilion and damaged a door with his bat.

He has strong views about apartheid in South Africa. He often argues that those black cricketers who have gone there to play have been 'used'. Viv would be a great propaganda capture for the South Africans, if they could tempt him. They have tried. On one occasion, he turned down an offer to play there for payment in the region of a quarter of a million pounds. 'Truth to my principles was worth more. There will have to be drastic improvements for the black man in South Africa before I even consider changing my mind,' said Viv.

1982 was Viv's benefit year. A brochure, containing

many tributes to his skill as a player and his personal qualities, was published. The contributor who pleased him the most was Lester B Bird, then Deputy Prime Minister of Antigua:

'Vivi had arrived on the cricket scene when his country was severely divided politically. The country needed a focal point which could form the basis of communal unity in a common cause . . . When he triumphed, the nation rejoiced. When he failed the nation mourned.

'I believe that Vivi's greatest contribution to his country was his affinity to and rapport with the youths of the nation, especially those from the area where he grew up. Whenever he returned, he never failed to socialise with them, to let them see he had not forgotten his roots . . . He was a stabilising force at a time when politics threatened to disrupt the fabric of our society.'

Viv Richards may once have been out for three ducks in a match, and earned a severe ticking off for it, but he has put Antigua on the map, in a way that no one else has. His blazing bat has done more than any room full of statesmen or public relations officers.

In his first season as a county cricketer in England, he was asked to name his greatest ambition. He thought for a moment and the answer had nothing to do with scoring personal centuries or even playing for the West Indies. 'I should love one day to see a Test Match played on my home ground at St. John's. That would prove we'd made it at last and were recognised as a

The Recreation Ground in St John's, Antigua

cricketing force,' he said. It was, of course, an ambition he more than realised when Antigua was granted its first official Test Match against England in 1981.

Viv Richards, then, is a person of contradictions — the joyful, flamboyant batsman and the very private person; the cricketer of great charm, clouded by occasional anger; the smiling, boyish, carefree newcomer to Somerset in 1974 and the sad-faced silent man saying goodbye to his friends at Taunton in 1986.

There are, however, no contradictions when it comes to his cricket. When the heart, the eye and the muscle are perfectly attuned, Viv Richards gives a performance of near-genius. Future generations will talk about him with awe and wish they had seen him play.

Important Dates in Viv Richards' Career

1971-72	Debut for Leeward Islands
1973	Arrives in England, to qualify for Somerset
1974	Debut for Somerset
1974	Awarded county cap
1974-75	Test debut for West Indies (against India)
1976	Two double centuries against England (232 at Trent Bridge and 291 at the Oval)
1977	Three double centuries for Somerset (against Gloucestershire, Sussex and Surrey)
1979	Scores 117 for Somerset in victorious Gillette Cup final against Northants
1981	Century to coincide with Antigua's first Test Match in St John's
1981	Scores 132 not out in Benson and Hedges final against Surrey
1981-82	Takes 5-88 against Queensland
1982	Benefit year for Somerset (£56,440)
1984-85	Succeeds Clive Lloyd as West Indies Captain
1985	Creates batting record for his county by scoring 322 against Warwickshire at Taunton
1986	Leaves Somerset amid controversy
1987	Joins Lancashire League side, Rishton

Viv Richards' Cricketing Achievements

Test Cricket

In 85 Tests Richards has scored 6,395 runs (average 53.74), taken 20 wickets and 20 catches.

He has scored 20 Test centuries, including three double centuries.

First Class Matches

In 392 matches Viv Richards has scored 28,809 runs (average 49.76), taken 178 wickets, 358 catches and made one stumping. He has scored 92 centuries.

He has scored 1000 runs in a season twelve times plus three times overseas.

Somerset Matches (First Class)

Since his debut in 1974, Richards has scored 14,698 runs (average 49.82), taken 96 wickets and 164 catches (including two as a wicket-keeper). He has scored 47 centuries including one triple century and five double centuries.

In 1986 he hit the fastest century of the season in 58 minutes, off 48 balls. This was against Glamorgan at Taunton.

His best season for the County was in 1977 when he scored 2,161 runs (average 65.48) with seven centuries.

He has hit six centuries before lunch for the County — two of them on the first day.

Limited Overs Matches (One Day)

Viv Richards has hit 146 sixes in the John Player League — a record.

In 1977 he hit 26 sixes in the John Player League — a record.

He has won six Gold Awards (Benson and Hedges Cup) and four Man of the Match Medals (Gillette Cup/Nat-West Trophy).

He completed the hat trick against Essex at Chelmsford (John Player League) in 1982.

(Statistics up to the end of 1986)